MW01482193

Liberty and Justice

TO DARE TO TELL THE TRUTH

The Story of Daniel Ellsberg

Written by Jason Nord

Illustrated by Reese Green

LINCOLN NEBRASKA

= EQUALITY PRESS =

Equality Press, Lincoln 68508

Copyright © 2015 by Jason Nord

All Rights Reserved. Published 2016.

Illustrations by Reese Green

Book design by Lacey Losh

Hardcover ISBN: 978-0-9905261-2-4
Paperback ISBN: 978-0-9905261-3-1

For more titles in the Liberty and Justice series, visit:

www.eqpress.org

Dan picked up his briefcase and walked out of his office. He tried to stay calm, but his heartbeat was pounding in his chest. If they caught him now, if they searched his briefcase, then everything would be over before it had even begun. The war would rage on, and the slaughter would continue. He needed to act naturally.

He reached forward and opened the door to the lobby. The security guards were sitting behind their desk just like they always were. The briefcase felt heavy as Dan walked past them.

"Goodnight, Dan," the guards said, waving politely. Dan waved back as casually as he could.

As he left through the front doors of The Rand Corporation, the business where he'd been working for the last few years, Dan passed a series of posters with warnings printed on them. One of them said:

What you see here,

What you say here,

Let it be here,

Let it stay here.

Dan had no intentions whatsoever of following that advice.

Inside of Daniel Ellsberg's brown leather briefcase were hundreds of pages of top secret documents. These papers were so secret that even the president of the United States, Richard Nixon, didn't know that they existed. They were so secret that only a handful of people on the entire planet had ever read them all.

Dan was one of those people. And the things that he had learned, the secrets he had discovered, had shocked him.

Dan's plan was to copy those top secret papers and share them with the rest of the world. He was tired of all the secrets. He was tired of all the lies. People were dying, lives were being destroyed, and the American people deserved to know the truth.

Dan knew that he would probably be arrested for what he was doing. He knew that he'd likely spend the rest of his life in prison for helping to end this war in Vietnam.

But Dan also knew that there are some things worth going to prison for.

To understand why Daniel Ellsberg would risk losing his freedom, would risk being separated from his friends and family for the rest of his life, it is important to understand America's war in Vietnam.

The country of Vietnam is long and slender. It stretches from north to south along the rocky coastline of Southeast Asia. It is filled with thick and beautiful jungles, jagged mountain ranges, and lush fields where farmers grow crops like rice, corn, and sweet potatoes.

But this gorgeous country has suffered a bloody history.   In the middle of the 1800s the French empire invaded Vietnam, dominating the people and taking control of the land. The French stole Vietnam's natural resources – the rice from the fields, the rubber from the forests, the tin deposits that lay buried in the mountains. Then, during World War II, the Japanese invaded, kicking the French out of power and taking Vietnam for themselves. The Japanese rule caused a brutal famine that killed more than a million people. After World War II ended, France invaded Vietnam again. Throughout all of this time – almost a hundred years – the Vietnamese people had been fighting for their independence. They dreamed of a day when the Vietnamese people would be free.

CHINA

CHINA

VIETNAM

MYANMAR
(BURMA)

LAOS

THAILAND

SOUTH
CHINA
SEA

CAMBODIA

VIETNAM

7

In 1954 the French government decided to pull all of its soldiers out of Vietnam. The French people were tired of a war that was killing its young men and costing their society huge amounts of money. Leaders in the American government began to panic; they were afraid that, if the Vietnamese people were allowed to hold elections and choose their own leaders, they would choose a government that the United States wouldn't like, perhaps even a government that would ally itself with America's enemy, a country called the U.S.S.R. American officials decided that the United States would use military force to stop this from happening.

The American invasion started small, but by the middle of the 1960s, hundreds of thousands of American soldiers were living in the southern half of Vietnam. They had the most advanced weaponry money could buy: tanks, grenade launchers, helicopters, fighter jets. They had fire bombs filled with napalm – a sticky substance that burns so hot it will even burn under water. They had toxic chemicals that they could spray from airplanes and helicopters, poisoning the land and killing all of the plant life, making it impossible for the Vietnamese people to hide in the jungles or eat food from the fields. They had 500-pound bombs that could destroy entire buildings, leaving nothing behind but a gigantic crater.

In contrast, the Vietnamese soldiers who fought against the Americans often had to fight with whatever they could find. Soldiers in the northern half of the country had plenty of modern weaponry, but most of the ground fighting took place in the southern part of Vietnam. Vietnamese soldiers moved weapons thousands of miles to the people fighting in the south on a long series of roads called the Ho Chi Min Trail.

But even with the supplies coming down the Ho Chi Min Trail, the fighters in the south often had to make do with very little. If they didn't have shoes for their feet, they wore sandals made from worn-out truck tires. If machine guns weren't available, they fought with old French rifles left over from the previous war. They made hand grenades by filling empty Coke cans with gunpowder from unexploded American bombs. They dug miles of underground tunnels where they could live and hide from American soldiers. They built traps out of sharpened bamboo spears or homemade explosives.

The one thing that the Vietnamese people had a lot of was determination. They were tired of other countries invading their homeland and telling them how to live. They were willing to fight and die for a world where Vietnam could be its own country and make its own laws.

Daniel Ellsberg first came to Vietnam as an employee of the United States government. Dan had served as a United States Marine officer, earned his doctorate degree from Harvard University, and spent much of his adult life studying how people make decisions during wartime. He had come to Vietnam to observe the war, to study it, so that he could give advice to government leaders back in Washington, D.C. He did many different things while he lived in Vietnam; he worked with the American ambassador, interviewed military officers, talked with Vietnamese residents, and marched in the fields with American soldiers.

During his time in Vietnam, Dan saw many things that deeply troubled him. He watched from an airplane as an entire village was destroyed by American bombs. He saw large areas of land that had once been thick jungles turned into lifeless deserts by the poisons dropped from American planes. He visited hospitals and met children with burns across their bodies from the napalm that had been dropped on their homes. He saw American soldiers fire their machine guns straight into people's houses before burning an entire village to the ground.

One day when Dan was driving through the Vietnamese countryside, he came to a village that was still burning from a recent attack. The surviving members of the village were digging through the ashes of their destroyed homes, searching for photographs or other valuable relics that hadn't been destroyed. Dan watched as children poked through the ruins, looking for their lost toys. One small girl clutched tightly to a plastic doll that had been blackened by the flames. Even years later, when Dan would think back to that day, it would make him cry.

The more that Dan learned about the war in Vietnam, the more he became convinced that it wasn't helping anyone. The United States had created a government for the citizens of South Vietnam, but a majority of the Vietnamese people didn't want that government; it was stealing money from the people and imprisoning citizens who disagreed with it. Most of the Vietnamese people just wanted America to leave them alone, and the American troops could feel it; they had been told by the president that they would be fighting to bring freedom to the Vietnamese people, but when the soldiers arrived in Vietnam, most people just treated them like invaders.

After living in Vietnam for nearly two years, studying the war and the Vietnamese people, Dan returned to live in the United States. He was offered a job with the Rand Corporation, a business that studies top secret documents and gives advice to government leaders. He left Vietnam convinced that the war was unwinnable, and that the wisest thing would be for the United States to leave Vietnam as quickly as possible.

Dan returned to an America that was deeply divided. While United States bombers were ravaging the Vietnamese countryside, more and more of the American people had become angry about the violence. They took to the streets by the thousands, holding massive protests, demanding an end to the war.

Many Americans were angry about something called "the draft." The draft was a system used by the United States government to force people to go to war. Every young man in America needed to register for the draft after his eighteenth birthday. After registering, the men were given a small piece of paper called a draft card that they had to carry with them at all times. The government then selected men from the group of everyone who

had registered and told them that they had to go fight. If you were selected and you refused to go fight, then the government could arrest you and send you to prison.

Thousands of young men resisted the draft, holding large demonstrations and chanting the slogan, "Hell No, We Won't Go!" They burned their draft cards as a way of showing the world that they wouldn't cooperate with a war that they thought was wrong. Many of these young men were arrested and sent to jail. Others fled the country, sneaking over the border into Canada where they would be safe from a government that was giving them an impossible choice: either go to war or go to prison.

Many people from the civil rights movement joined this anti-war movement. Martin Luther King, Jr. – the famous civil rights leader and winner of the Nobel Peace Prize – gave a speech entitled "Why I Oppose the Vietnam War." In it he compared America to "a society gone mad on war." He went on to call the United States government "the greatest purveyor of violence in the world today." He was saddened that the country was willing to spend billions of dollars on bombs and missiles while poor Americans were suffering and their country did little to help them.

Many of the young men who fought in the war came home very sad about what they'd seen. Some of them formed a group called "Vietnam Veterans Against the War." They held large demonstrations where they talked about the horrible things that they had witnessed – and in many cases, the horrible things that they had done – during their time in Vietnam. At one demonstration, thousands of former soldiers gathered around the Capitol building in Washington, D.C. They took turns giving short speeches, and then they threw their war medals over the fence. They didn't want awards for fighting against the Vietnamese people.

While anti-war protests swept across the country, Daniel spent his days studying top secret documents, trying to understand everything that was happening in Vietnam. Then one day his life was changed forever when he met a young peace activist named Janaki.

Janaki was from southern India. She explained to him that in her culture people didn't believe in "enemies." For Dan, a man who had studied warfare for most of his life, this was an amazing idea. Janaki explained that everyone had goodness in them, even if sometimes they might do evil things. She believed in peacefully resisting violence, even if it meant sacrificing your own life to help make the world a better place. She introduced him to the teachings of philosophers like Mahatma Gandhi and Henry David Thoreau.

Dan was interested, and he wanted to learn more. In 1969, Janaki invited him to an anti-war conference in Philadelphia. He met two young men there that he liked very much: Bob Eaton and Randy Kehler. Both of them were intelligent, thoughtful, and kind. Both of them had worked hard for years in the anti-war movement. Both of them were going to prison soon; they had been drafted by the government, and they were refusing to go to war.

Randy was giving a speech at the conference; people from all over the world packed into an auditorium to hear him talk. Dan sat in the very back row. Randy spoke about living a life devoted to peace, about helping to build a new society that could be more compassionate, more equal, more like an extended family. He said that he wasn't afraid of going to prison, because he knew that the people in that auditorium would continue struggling every day to end the war and make the world a better place.

When Randy's speech was over, people shot to their feet, cheering. Applause thundered through the room. Dan stood and clapped, but then he fell backwards into his chair, overcome by emotion. Tears were streaming down his face. He needed to get away, to be by himself. He exited through the back of the auditorium.

Dan ducked into the nearest bathroom, then collapsed to the floor, sobbing. He wept uncontrollably as thoughts ricocheted inside his head. He thought of all of the horrible things that he had seen in Vietnam: the people killed, the homes destroyed, the children with burns all over their bodies. He thought of young men like Bob Eaton and Randy Kehler – amazing and brave Americans who would be locked up in prison simply because they didn't want to kill people. He thought of the American soldiers with whom he'd fought side by side. Many of them would die in Vietnam and would never be able to live and have families and grow old. He thought of his own son, Robert, who someday would be old enough for the draft, who someday might need to make that terrible decision: go to war or go to prison.

Dan cried and cried because he knew in his heart and in his mind that this war in Vietnam was evil. It was an act of mass murder that was destroying Vietnam and a whole generation of America's youth. It needed to be stopped.

After weeping for about an hour, Dan picked himself up and cleaned himself off. He knew that he needed to do something to help end the war. He would go to prison if he had to; he wasn't afraid of that. The only question that remained was, "What could he do?"

As the weeks passed, Dan began to find an answer to that question. As part of his job, Dan had been reading a top secret history of the Vietnam War. This document, which was 7,000 pages long, showed over and over again that four different American presidents had all lied to the American people about what was happening in Vietnam.

Over and over again presidents had claimed that America was fighting to support democracy and freedom in Vietnam. In reality the secret history showed that the American government had stopped free elections while supporting dictators who imprisoned and tortured anybody who disagreed with them.

Over and over again American presidents had claimed that they were trying to end the war. Yet, while the presidents claimed that they were working towards peace, they were secretly making plans for more bombings and bigger invasions. American forces had even attacked two of Vietnam's neighbors, Laos and Cambodia, without the American people knowing about it.

Even the beginning of the war had been a lie. President Lyndon Johnson had told the American people that the Vietnamese had attacked America first. In fact the United States had been secretly blowing up bridges and railroads, kidnapping Vietnamese soldiers, and placing landmines in Vietnamese roadways long before the people of Vietnam had begun to fight back.

As Dan read more and more of the top secret history, he began to view the whole American government as a "lying machine." He was tired of it; he decided he would copy the top secret history and share it with everyone in the world. Maybe if the American people knew the truth about the war – about all the lies that they'd been told – then the anti-war movement would grow and the American people could force their own government to bring an end to the bloodshed.

Knowing that it would take a long time to copy 7,000 pages of top secret documents, Dan asked his friend Tony Russo to help him. Tony had once worked for the Rand Corporation, but he'd been fired for writing reports that his bosses didn't like – reports that talked about some of the horrible things that had been done to the Vietnamese people. Tony agreed to help Dan right away, and he even mentioned that he had a friend named Lynda Sinay who was opposed to the war and would be happy to let them use her copying machine.

And so Dan began smuggling documents out of The Rand Corporation in his brown leather suitcase. On that first night, after passing by the guards without being searched, Dan hopped into his car and met up with Tony and Lynda. Lynda led them into her office and taught them how to disable the alarm system. Then, while Tony and Lynda talked in the next room, Dan began making copies of the top secret history.

He'd only been working for a brief while when somebody began knocking on the office door. Dan turned his head to look; two police officers were standing outside.

One of them had his nightstick out and was using it to bang on the glass door. The policeman gestured with his other hand, telling Dan to open the door and let them in.

Dan closed the lid of the copying machine so that the page labeled TOP SECRET would be hidden from sight. For the second time that night, he fought to keep himself calm. "How did they find us so quickly?" he asked himself.

Dan opened the door, expecting to be arrested. "Can I help you officers?"

"Your alarm is going off," said one of the policemen.

Dan called for Lynda, who was in the other room. She greeted the policemen happily and explained that she must have turned the alarm off incorrectly. The police officers joked with her– apparently she had done this before– and Lynda promised to take lessons on how to use her alarm system properly. Finally the policemen wished them all a good night and walked away into the darkness.

Dan worked until dawn that first night. In the many months that followed, Dan barely ever slept; he went to work during the day-time and copied documents at night. He said goodbye to his ex-wife and to his children, Robert and Mary, knowing that he'd likely be in prison soon and wouldn't be able to see them. It broke his heart to leave them behind, but millions of people were dying in this war. Dan knew that he had to do everything in his power to help make the killing stop.

At first Dan gave copies of the top secret history to several different United States senators, hoping that once they learned about the lies they would use their power to help bring an end to the war. As months went by, and the senators did nothing, Dan decided to begin showing the top secret documents to the newspapers.

On June 13, 1971, the New York Times newspaper began publishing sections of the top secret history. People were amazed and outraged by what they read. TV stations held long discussions about the lies that the presidents had told. Each day the New York Times printed more and more of the documents. People began calling the secret history "The Pentagon Papers."

People in President Nixon's office were not happy. They ordered the New York Times to stop printing the Pentagon Papers. It was the first time in the history of the United States of America that the government had ever banned a newspaper from being able to publish the truth.

Though this was unfortunate, Dan wasn't going to let it stop him. If the government was going to ban the New York Times from publishing the secret history, then Dan would just have to go to a different newspaper.   He made an appointment to meet secretly with a reporter from a newspaper called the Washington Post.

Dan and his wife, Patricia, met the reporter at a hotel room. They exchanged two huge boxes of top secret documents and prepared to go their separate ways. But before leaving the hotel room, Dan and Patricia happened to turn on the TV. They saw their own house in front of them on the glowing screen. FBI agents were on their front porch, knocking on the door. The television announcer said that the FBI was looking for a man named Daniel Ellsberg.

Though Dan had always known that he would likely be arrested, he wasn't willing to give up quite yet. He still had more copies of the Pentagon Papers, and he wanted to get them delivered to as many newspapers as possible before he had to go to jail.

He and Patricia decided to go into hiding. On that first night, they checked into a hotel using fake names. They had no extra clothing, no toothbrushes, no shaving cream, none of the normal comforts of home. But they did have access to thousands of pages of top secret documents and a strong desire to share the truth with the American people.

Over the next twelve days the FBI searched throughout the country and across the world trying desperately to catch Daniel Ellsberg. Patricia and Dan moved frequently, just in case they were being followed. They had friends who were willing to help them hide, and many complete strangers opened up their homes, allowing Dan and Patricia to sleep in their basements. All of these people were risking their own freedom, but they didn't care; they were proud to be helping the man who was trying to end the war in Vietnam.

On one occasion the police almost caught Dan and Patricia. They were hiding out in a second-floor apartment in Cambridge, Massachusetts. A friend of theirs had recently left to go make a phone call at a payphone across the street. He was helping Dan and Patricia contact reporters who might want copies of the Pentagon Papers.

Dan and Patricia watched their friend through the apartment window as he finished his phone call. Hanging up the receiver, he turned, crossed the street, and reentered the apartment building.

Just then four police cars came screaming into view. They

slammed to a halt, their tires screeching. Police officers erupted from the doors of the vehicles, their guns gripped tightly in their hands. Noticing that the phone booth was empty, they spread out and began searching the nearby streets.

Dan and Patricia dropped to the floor so that the police couldn't see them through the windows. Apparently the FBI was spying on people's phone conversations in an attempt to catch the two fugitives. It had been a close call; if their friend had stayed on the phone for only a minute longer, he would have been caught, and their hiding place might have been discovered.

While Dan and Patricia were in hiding, they kept delivering copies of the Pentagon Papers to reporters from across the nation. Soon dozens of different newspapers were printing pieces of the top secret history. Though the government tried to stop a few of them, the stories kept flooding out into the public. The truth had become unstoppable.

Meanwhile, everyone in the country was talking about the Pentagon Papers. Every news show on television spent most of its time each night discussing the documents and the lies that they exposed. Time magazine – one of the most popular magazines in America – put a picture of Dan on their front cover while he and Patricia were still in hiding. Around the same time, a man named Walter Cronkite – perhaps the most famous news broadcaster in the world – offered to interview Dan at a secret location. While the FBI was scouring the country, desperately trying to find Dan's hiding place, Dan went on national television and talked with Walter about the need to end the Vietnam War.

Having delivered all of his copies of the Pentagon Papers, Dan decided it was time to turn himself in. He announced to the world that he would come out of hiding at the main post office of the city of Boston on the morning of Monday, June 28, 1971.

When that morning finally came, Dan put on his very best suit. He thought about what he would say to the reporters when he got there. Then he and Patricia got into a taxi and drove to the post office to meet the police.

The square in front of the Post Office Building was packed from end to end with people, many of whom were carrying signs supporting Daniel Ellsberg. When Dan and Patricia stepped out of the taxi, the crowd erupted in cheers. To the many people across the country who were tired of the war, tired of the killing, and tired of the lies, Dan had become a hero. They had come out to congratulate him, to welcome him, and to thank him.

As the reporters gathered around, Dan gave a short speech explaining why he had released the Pentagon Papers. In his speech he expressed his hope that the American people, armed with the truth, would demand that their presidents stop lying to them and that their government end the brutal bloodshed in Vietnam.

After his speech was over, a reporter asked Dan if he had any concerns about going to prison.

Without pausing, Dan looked at him and said:

"Wouldn't you go to prison to help end this war?"

Dan was arrested, and in the months that followed he was charged with 12 different crimes. If a jury found him guilty, he could be sentenced to 115 years in prison. The police also arrested Tony Russo, who faced the possibility of 25 years in jail.

Meanwhile, the Supreme Court of the United States – the most powerful court in America – ruled that the New York Times and other newspapers could continue to publish the Pentagon Papers. The court's message was clear: nobody, not even the president, had the right to stop newspapers from publishing the truth.

With America watching, Daniel Ellsberg and Tony Russo were put on trial for releasing top secret documents. The courtroom drama quickly became almost as shocking as the Pentagon Papers themselves. Evidence came forward that the FBI had illegally used wiretaps to spy on Dan's friends. Furthermore, it was discovered that the president himself, Richard Nixon, had ordered men to illegally break into Dan's psychiatrist's office. The president had also tried to bribe the judge in Dan's case by offering him a position as the head of the FBI.

On the morning of May 11, 1973, the judge announced that both Daniel Ellsberg and Tony Russo would be set free. The government had broken too many laws and lied too many times for Dan and Tony to have a chance at a fair trial.

The courtroom exploded with excitement: people cheered, people laughed, people cried out of happiness. In the middle of all of the chaos, Dan and Patricia found each other. They kissed each other passionately. Dan had been willing to go to prison for the rest of his life, but he'd be much happier being able to live and grow old with the woman that he loved.

In the months that followed, the United States Congress voted to ban any further combat operations in Vietnam. America's invasion of Vietnam officially ended on May 1, 1975.

The war in Vietnam had been long and deadly. Almost sixty thousand American soldiers had died in the conflict. More than two million Vietnamese citizens – men and women, children and adults – had been killed by American bombs and American bullets. The United States had dropped more explosives on the country of Vietnam than had ever been dropped on any other nation in the history of the world.

Yet, through all of this tragedy, we can see hope. Thanks to the work of people like Daniel Ellsberg, Patricia Ellsberg, Tony Russo, Lynda Sinay, Bob Eaton, Randy Kehler, Janaki, and the thousands upon thousands of anti-war activists whose names we'll never know, a war had been stopped. These people showed us that, with enough passion, enough effort, enough bravery, and enough sacrifice, we can work together to forge a more peaceful planet, one where honesty and respect become the foundations of our society.

References

Ellsberg, Daniel. Secrets: A Memoir of Vietnam and the Pentagon Papers. New York: Penguin Books, 2003. Print.

Mangold, Tom, and John Penycate. The Tunnels of Cu Chi. New York: Berkley Books, 1986. Print.

Palmer, Michael G. "The Case of Agent Orange." Contemporary Southeast Asia. 29.1 (2007): 172-95. Web. 31 July. 2013.

The Most Dangerous Man in America: Daniel Ellsberg and the Pentagon Papers, produced and directed by Judith Ehrlich and Rick Goldsmith, 2009. DVD distributed by First Run Features.

"Vietnam Veterans Memorial." Columbia Electronic Encyclopedia. 6th ed. 2013. Web. 30 July. 2013.

Young, Marilyn B. The Vietnam Wars 1945-1990. New York: Harper Perennial, 1991. Print.

Young, Marilyn B. "The War's Tragic Legacy." Major Problems in the History of the Vietnam War. Ed. Robert J. McMahon. Lexington, Massachusetts: D. C. Heath and Company, 1995. 637-647. Print.

Zinn, Howard. A People's History of the United States. New York: Harper Perennial, 2005. Print.

CPSIA information can be obtained at www.ICGtesting.com
Printed in the USA
LVIW01n1926030616
491162LV00002B/2